SUMMARY & ANALYSIS

OF

WHITE FRAGILITY

WHY IT'S SO HARD

FOR **WHITE PEOPLE** TO

TALK ABOUT RACISM

A GUIDE TO THE BOOK
BY ROBIN DiANGELO

BY ZIPREADS

NOTE: This book is a summary and analysis and is meant as a companion to, not a replacement for, the original book.
Please follow this link to purchase a copy of the original book: https://amzn.to/2O3Zi2c

TABLE OF CONTENTS

SYNOPSIS

In her book *White Fragility: Why It's So Hard for White People to Talk about Racism*, Robin J. DiAngelo explores the idea that white Americans are socialized to keep silent on race issues. This inhibits their ability to tolerate any discussion on racial equality and justice. The result is that white people often become defensive or argumentative when their racist assumptions are openly challenged.

White fragility is defined as "a state in which even a minimum amount of racial stress becomes intolerable, triggering a range of defensive moves." When a white person is challenged about a racist idea or statement they have made, they often lash out or withdraw, claiming that they are not racist. The problem is that many white people believe that racism is an event that is perpetuated by an evil person, but this is not true.

Racism is a system and structure that pervades every facet of American society, and all white people are silent beneficiaries of this system. This means that you can be a good person but still hold racist views. DiAngelo contends that white people do this all the time without even realizing it.

The author recommends white people must learn to tolerate conversations about racism without getting defensive or apathetic. White people must deeply examine their lives and begin to challenge their racist assumptions.

CHAPTER SUMMARIES & KEY TAKEAWAYS

CHAPTER 1: THE CHALLENGES OF TALKING TO WHITE PEOPLE ABOUT RACISM

DiAngelo delves into the main challenges that she faces when trying to get white people to talk about racism. She identifies four main issues that most white people hide behind when faced with a question on race. These challenges include race identity, uninformed opinions, socialization, and the simplification of what being a "racist" really means.

Key Takeaway: White people do not perceive themselves to be racist.

As a white person, DiAngelo points out that her life experiences, worldview, and frame of reference are all intrinsically white. She argues that she, like every other white person, was raised to disregard her skin color and not to use her race as an advantage. For this reason, white people rarely discuss issues of race, especially their own.

Yet in American society, race is a major issue because of the existence of profound racial inequality. DiAngelo contends that if this racial inequality is to be tackled, white people must learn to act as if race does matter. If you are white, you need to "name your race, "as uncomfortable as it may be.

Key Takeaway: Though white people have strong opinions on race, these beliefs are often ignorant.

According to DiAngelo, every white person she has met has a strong opinion of racism. However, she argues that white people have *uninformed* opinions on race because they rely on information that is skewed against people of color. Mainstream American culture and the media are filled with social forces that constantly try to push a certain narrative about racism.

When the topic of racism is brought up, white people either clam up or become defensive and argumentative. Such responses prevent white people from gaining deeper knowledge about racism. The result is that racist frameworks continue to be perpetuated.

Key Takeaway: To understand white fragility, you need to understand socialization.

White people tend to respond in a similar way when asked about racism. This is because of their shared culture and socialization. There are two ideologies that prevent white people from seeing how their culture clouds their racial viewpoint: individuality and objectivity.

In the West, you are taught to believe that your individual character is more relevant than your social group. Therefore, if racism is perpetuated by individuals and not groups, it's not your problem. However, DiAngelo argues that racism is a group problem. Children are subliminally taught that some groups are better than others, and therefore, you are better off belonging to one group than another. White people are also taught that having an opinion of racism is biased, and therefore, they refuse to examine their own viewpoints. You cannot understand racism if you refuse to explore how group culture affects individuals.

Key Takeaway: You need to understand the true definition of "racist."

Most people believe that a racist is an immoral person who hates others due to their race. When white people are accused of being racist, they disagree because they don't see themselves conforming to this definition. However, DiAngelo claims that this definition isn't accurate. To overcome white fragility, white people must accept the discomfort of learning what racism truly means.

CHAPTER 2: RACISM AND WHITE SUPREMACY

Contrary to what you were taught, different races are not genetically or biologically different. Differences in skin, hair, and eye color are simply geographical adaptations. Therefore, race is a social construct, just like gender. DiAngelo explains how economic and social forces continue to conspire to divide society along racial lines.

Key Takeaway: Racism was created to justify economic exploitation of people of color. (and poor whites)

Though America was formed on the principles of freedom and equality, its economy was built on African slavery, Native American genocide, and annexation of Mexico. In order to justify the unequal treatment of people of color, scientists sought to prove that they were naturally inferior to the whites. Therefore, they created a narrative of black genetic inferiority to divert attention away from systemic discrimination.

Key Takeaway: It is white people who decided who was white or not.   — men

Prior to the 1600s, the concept of "white" didn't exist. The term was introduced through colonial law. When European immigrants began arriving en masse, people like the Irish, Italians, Armenians, and Polish were not classified as white. To avoid exclusion, they had to petition the courts, where white men would decide which groups were white or not.

Since race is a social construct, even poor, white Americans were regarded as second-class citizens. To prevent working-class whites from protesting against the ruling elite, they were granted full whiteness. As long as they felt superior to people of color, they wouldn't focus on the true cause of their poverty.

Key Takeaway: Racism can only be perpetuated by those who hold power.

There is a difference between prejudice, discrimination, and racism. Prejudice occurs when you prejudge others based on their social group. Discrimination occurs when action is taken to back up prejudice, for example, threats and violence. Racism, however, is defined as a structure or system that is supported by institutional, legal, and social power.

Though people of color may be prejudiced against whites, they do not have the means (laws and policies) to implement their discrimination throughout society. In the US, white people control all the instruments of power, and therefore, only they can exercise racial privilege over other races.

CHAPTER 3: RACISM AFTER THE CIVIL RIGHTS MOVEMENT

Though many white Americans believe that racism has ended, it still exists in a more implicit and adaptive form. DiAngelo reviews how racism has changed over time such that white people today no longer sense their involvement in this oppressive system.

Key Takeaway: Racism can be color-blind.

Color-blind racism occurs when you refute the existence of racism by pretending not to notice skin color. During the

Civil Rights movement, white people were shocked to see how black people were being brutalized. After King's famous speech, many white people assumed that as long as they didn't acknowledge someone's race, then racism would automatically end.

However, pretending not to see color means you project your reality onto the other person. For example, if a white person feels well-treated at work, then surely their black coworker feels the same way. Color-blind racism prevents you from addressing your negative unconscious beliefs about the other race

Key Takeaway: You can be racist while claiming plausible deniability.

DiAngelo provides an example of how some of her white friends and coworkers advised her not to get a home in specific neighborhoods due to perceived insecurity. On further investigation, she discovered that all these "unsafe" areas were predominantly black or brown. She believes that this is aversive racism, where white people use coded language to make racist statements without appearing overtly racist. Aversive racism is subtle and allows you to maintain a positive self-image.

Key Takeaway: Racism is accepted as part of white culture.

DiAngelo explains how white millennials are still practicing racism but are simply hiding the fact. She provides examples of how white college students make blatantly racist remarks when in all-white company, but then become racially conscious when people of color are around. Studies show that cultural racism is ingrained at childhood, and therefore, millennials are just as racist as previous generations.

CHAPTER 4: HOW DOES RACE SHAPE THE LIVES OF WHITE PEOPLE?

Why are white people uncomfortable with having conversations about race? DiAngelo reveals the aspects that white fragility is founded upon. These aspects cannot apply to a person of color.

Key Takeaway: You grow up with a sense of belonging.

A white child is born feeling like they belong to the dominant culture. Their parents have access to a good hospital with white doctors; the school has white teachers; the movies have white actors, and the books are written by white authors. As they grow up, they never have to think about their race because belonging is a natural occurrence.

The only time they feel like they don't belong is when associating with people of color.

Key Takeaway: You never have to worry about your race.

A white person never has to worry about how their skin color is perceived unless they are attending an event hosted by people of color. They can work in any organization and in any field without even considering whether their skin color will matter. DiAngelo argues that a white person would never have been stopped by George Zimmerman.

Key Takeaway: You can go wherever you want to.

A white person enjoys the freedom of movement and can visit any place that they choose. DiAngelo recollects how a black associate of hers refused to holiday in northern Idaho because the Aryan Nation had an encampment in the area. Furthermore, her coworker felt that the white people would isolate her because they may not have interacted with a black person before.

CHAPTER 5: THE GOOD/BAD BINARY

The good/bad binary refers to a variation of racism that has cropped up in recent times. Before the 1960s, white people didn't have a problem being racist. But after the Civil Rights Movement, northern whites began to view racism as an immoral, southern problem. Therefore, white people created a dichotomy where as long as you were good/moral, then you couldn't be racist. DiAngelo provides examples to show that this isn't true.

Key Takeaway: Many white people believe that racism is a character flaw.

When a white person is called a racist, they assume that it's an attack on their character and morality. They try to defend their character and stop the conversation instead of examining their actions. DiAngelo argues that this is wrong because racism and morality are not mutually exclusive. You can be a good person yet still conform to the system and structure that perpetuates racism. As long as white people refuse to challenge the system, racism will continue.

Key Takeaway: You can be racist without realizing it.

DiAngelo explains how a white teacher in one of her presentations mimicked a parent who had been protesting against the school system. Everyone in the room, including her white colleagues, could tell that she was mocking an angry black woman. When confronted about her racial mockery and stereotyping, she grew defensive and quit the session.

When white people are confronted about their racist behavior, they resort to specific statements to prove their good character. They say things like:

- I have black friends/coworkers

- My parents weren't racist; they taught me to treat everybody the same

- I grew up poor in a diverse neighborhood

- I lived as a minority in Africa

- This is not about race

- Talking about racism divides people

These statements may be logical, but they do not prove that your actions aren't racist in nature. Racism is so deep into American society that white people often fail to see it.

CHAPTER 6: ANTI-BLACKNESS

There are many different groups of color in America, such as blacks, indigenous and Asian. However, white people don't see themselves as a group but rather as unique individuals. While all groups of color may experience racism, whites tend to consider black people as their major "adversary." DiAngelo claims that to challenge racism, white people must also view themselves as a group that is socialized to be anti-black.

Key Takeaway: Without blackness, there would be no white identity.

DiAngelo claims that "white is a false identity." You can only be white if there is someone who isn't white. Therefore, whiteness cannot exist without blackness. White people need black people so that they can have a target for a unified hatred. For white people to feel superior in their identity, they must create the narrative that black people are inferior.

This is how whites justify the enslavement of blacks and their aversion to blackness. Whites then project the things they hate about themselves onto black people. For example, blacks are described as lazy and violent, yet they are the ones who toiled daily in plantation farms and suffered immense brutality at the hands of whites.

Key Takeaway: Of all the people of color, it is blacks who are most despised by whites.

Studies show that white flight occurs in a neighborhood when black families begin to move in. Most white Americans say that they can tolerate up to thirty percent of blacks in a neighborhood, but actual movement patterns show that when the population of a neighborhood reaches seven percent black, whites start to move out.

In 2015, the American Sociological Foundation revealed that whites prefer Asians and then Latinos in their neighborhoods. The study showed that the biggest segregation occurs between whites and blacks.

Key Takeaway: Guilt makes whites dehumanize blacks.

DiAngelo states that whites know the historical mistreatment they have meted out on blacks. This guilt is traumatic, and many whites suppress it by trying to justify these brutal actions. By painting black people as non-human, whites can then blame the victims and convince themselves that blacks deserved the brutality they received. This is evident in the way whites keep silent when blacks are depicted as apes in the media and executed by the police without just cause.

CHAPTER 7: RACIAL TRIGGERS FOR WHITE PEOPLE

According to DiAngelo, being white provides you with certain privileges, status, and resources. This produces a situation where white people are protected from any form of racial discomfort or stress. They rarely have to consider issues of race, and even when they do, it's in some kind of college course or workplace training. Therefore, when whites are openly challenged about racial realities, it triggers white fragility. DiAngelo describes the main aspects that explain white fragility.

Key Takeaway: White fragility responses are subconscious yet predictable.

DiAngelo uses Bourdieu's theory to explain how white fragility works. The theory incorporates three aspects: *field, capital, and habitus*. Field refers to the social context in which you exist, for example, school or the workplace. Capital refers to your social value—a receptionist has greater capital than a janitor. Habitus refers to your awareness of your status and how you respond to the status of others. It depends on social cues that must be followed and is determined by whoever has the most capital in a specific field. When this social equilibrium is challenged, you subconsciously try to regain that balance.

When a white person feels that their position is challenged via racial stress, they engage in defensive behaviors to fix the equilibrium. They get angry, argumentative, feel guilty, fearful, keep silent, or leave the room. DiAngelo states that whites simply don't know how to respond constructively under racial stress. This leads them to display a predictable and reflexive behavior pattern to regain the capital they have lost.

CHAPTER 8: THE RESULT: WHITE FRAGILITY

Most whites believe that they are discriminated against in today's America, yet only a few can state whether they have ever experienced discrimination. DiAngelo contends that every time people of color bring up racial issues, whites respond as if they have been attacked. They act as if they have been traumatized and, therefore, the conversation should cease. This is a form of white bullying.

Key Takeaway: Whites engage in self-defense when challenged about racism.

The 2016 Oscars were marred by accusations of a failure to include black actors among the nominees for the second year running. Some white actors considered these accusations unfair and "racist against whites." DiAngelo points out that this is part of a self-defense pattern that whites engage in when racism crops up.

They see themselves as blamed, victimized, and attacked, even though there hasn't been any physical violence. By acting like victims, whites take attention off the issue and paint themselves as non-racists. The language used also shows how unprepared whites are when it comes to confronting racial tensions.

Key Takeaway: Whites claim that racial topics cause them trauma.

DiAngelo describes how some organizations warn her that the white employees have been traumatized by past attempts to diversify the workforce. One woman even claimed to be having a heart attack when she was told of how her statements had affected her fellow participants who were of color.

By claiming to be traumatized, whites discourage the leadership from addressing issues of lack of diversity. The goal is to change the topic and refocus the attention on something else. By claiming trauma, whites are seeking to stop any challenge to their entitlement. At the end of the day, the organization stays predominantly white.

Key Takeaway: White fragility leads to verbal incoherence.

One sociological study revealed that when whites talk about racial issues in public, their speech somehow becomes incomprehensible. This verbal incoherence manifests as self-corrections, long pauses, digressions, and repetition. This is because white people insist that race doesn't matter, and are thus unprepared to share their racial perspectives. According to DiAngelo, as long as whites are reluctant to talk about racism, the more they will continue to assume that the white perspective is the universal perspective.

CHAPTER 9: WHITE FRAGILITY IN ACTION

DiAngelo provides significant examples of how whites react when the topic of racial equity is brought up. She narrates how Eva, a white woman, claimed she couldn't be racist because she grew up in Germany and had never interacted with black people. DiAngelo challenged her claim by asking Eva whether she had ever watched films depicting African Americans or received messages about people in Africa. She was also asked how she related to blacks ever since she moved to the U.S.

Eva later approached DiAngelo in a furious rage and stated that she had been offended by her assumptions. This is despite the fact that nobody had called her a racist. From her experience, DiAngelo has learned that white fragility always follows a specific pattern.

Key Takeaway: When an assumption is challenged, it triggers an emotional reaction

Eva saw herself as someone who couldn't be racist because of her upbringing. DiAngelo, however, pointed out that living in isolation from black people doesn't mean you cannot hold negative views about blacks. When her assumed self-image was challenged, Eva reacted emotionally.

Some of the emotional reactions that define white fragility include feeling:

- Judged
- Accused
- Attacked
- Insulted
- Guilty
- Angry

Key Takeaway: The emotional reaction then triggers an expected behavior.

Once Eva felt overwhelmed by her emotions, she immediately exhibited a specific behavior pattern. White fragility usually leads to the following behaviors:

- Arguing
- Denying
- Avoiding
- Crying
- Seeking absolution
- Physically leaving

Key Takeaway: White fragility behaviors then trigger specific claims.

To justify their emotions and behavior, whites resort to making specific claims. These claims are meant to stop further engagement and avoid any kind of accountability.

Some of these claims include:

- You have hurt my feelings
- I am aware of all this
- I was misunderstood
- You are the one who is racist
- That's your opinion
- I have also suffered

- The problem isn't race, it's gender/class/etc.
- I don't like your tone
- I have black friends
- Some people get offended even when there is no offense
- I didn't mean that

Key Takeaway: White fragility serves several purposes

DiAngelo states that white fragility has the following functions:

- It trivializes racism
- It protects white privilege
- It prevents self-reflection
- It preserves white solidarity
- It paints whites as the victims
- It targets the messenger instead of the message

At the end of the day, white fragility protects racism.

CHAPTER 10: WHITE FRAGILITY AND THE RULES OF ENGAGEMENT

Through her years of experience with diversity training, DiAngelo has discovered that white people have a set of guidelines that they insist on before they accept feedback about racism. These unspoken rules are designed to protect white superiority and hide racism when it occurs.

Key Takeaway: When challenging white people about their racist assumptions, you have to follow certain rules.

These are the eleven unspoken rules that define white fragility:

1. Never offer feedback about my racism, no matter what – This is the cardinal rule. However, if you break this rule, then make sure to follow the others.

2. Use a proper tone – Provide feedback calmly. If you express emotions, then I will dismiss your feedback.

3. We have to trust one another – You must believe that I am not racist before you challenge my racism.

4. We must not have any pending issues between us – Before you challenge my racism, we must first resolve our unrelated issues.

5. You must provide the feedback immediately – If you don't, then I won't take it seriously.

6. Feedback must be given in private, even if the incident was in public – If you embarrass me in public, your feedback is unfounded and I am the victim.

7. Your feedback must be indirect – Otherwise, you are being insensitive to my feelings.

8. I need to feel safe when talking about race – If you say that my assumptions are racist, I won't feel safe. You can regain my trust by never challenging my racism again.

9. If you say I'm racist, then you are invalidating the oppression I went through (e.g. sexism, classism, etc) – Therefore, you are oppressing me.

10. You have to acknowledge that my intentions are always good – Even if my behavior is racist.

11. If you say my behavior is racist, then you misunderstood me – Let me explain my perspective so that you can admit *your* mistake.

DiAngelo points out that some of these rules are contradictory and unworkable. However, they serve their function well—to shut down any feedback on racism.

CHAPTER 11: WHITE WOMEN'S TEARS

White tears are a reference to the ways in which white people lament over the effects of racism on them. DiAngelo specifically talks about how white women shed tears in multi-racial settings. She contends that when white women cry, they divert attention away from the racial issue at hand. This antagonizes the people of color who are the actual victims of the racist incident.

Key Takeaway: White women's tears can reinforce racism.

DiAngelo describes a cross-racial community meeting that was called after the police shot an unarmed black man. Before the meeting, a woman of color told her that though she wanted to attend, she didn't feel like dealing with "white women's tears." DiAngelo then informed the white participants to refrain from crying during the meeting. Afterward, an extremely angry white woman asked her why she wasn't allowed to cry in front of people of color.

Most people assume that emotions are natural, but they are also political. Your tears are shaped by your biases, culture, and beliefs. Since women tend to cry more than men, and white people falsely believe that only evil people can be racist, then white women will resort to crying when their racist assumptions are exposed. In a multicultural setting, the white (and even black) men will rush to console the white woman. The person who has pointed out the white woman's racism is then demonized and everyone forgets about the people of color who were offended by the racism. Therefore, the tears of a white woman tend to reinforce racism.

Key Takeaway: People of color don't see white tears as solidarity.

When a white woman cries in a cross-cultural setting, she may assume that the people of color will share her feelings. The tears may be due to the shock of seeing a racist incident, but people of color see such tears as proof of racial insulation. If a white person doesn't have any genuine cross-racial relationships, then how can their tears (in a cross-racial setting) be a sign of solidarity with people they rarely interact with?

DiAngelo argues that white tears are the result of inner guilt and simply come across as being narcissistic. She narrates how a white woman was promoted to supervise an organization that deals with racial justice. The women of color in the organization, who had greater experience and had actually trained the new employee, were overlooked. The white woman stood in front of them shedding tears as she asked for their support. She didn't realize that her tears were covering up the fact that a racial justice organization had just reinforced racism.

CHAPTER 12: WHERE DO WE GO FROM HERE?

DiAngelo and her equity team meet with a web developer. The team includes two black women and the web developer is also black. When the web developer hands out survey forms, DiAngelo pushes the forms aside because she would rather explain herself verbally. During the conversation, she explains how one of her black colleagues was discriminated against during an antiracism training session. DiAngelo then jokes that it was her black colleague's braids that scared the white people. Later on, DiAngelo is informed that the web developer found the hair comment offensive. After consulting a white friend, DiAngelo meets with the web developer and they repair the relationship.

Key Takeaway: It is possible to transform your white paradigm.

White fragility manifests in the form of assumptions, emotions, behaviors, and claims. However, when DiAngelo made a racist comment, she was able to repair the relationship by interrupting her racist patterns. She changed her paradigm by expressing emotions, behaviors, and claims that are the opposite of white fragility.

Her emotions were:

- Gratitude
- Interest
- Compassion
- Humility

Her behavior was:

- Apology
- Engaging
- Reflection
- Listening

Some of her claims were:

- I appreciate your helpful feedback
- I need to work on myself

- My focus will be the message and not the messenger
- This conversation is difficult but important

Key Takeaway: White people can take steps to deal with white fragility.

White people can get educated about racism in a variety of ways. You can build relationships with people of color, but don't depend on them to teach you about racism. You should do your own research via books, films, and websites to learn how to end white apathy toward racism.

DiAngelo also recommends that you talk to another white person who will help you process rather than spare your feelings. If you are repairing a broken relationship, you should own your racism instead of making excuses. It is important to be racially aware and challenge fellow whites who practice racial arrogance.

Key Takeaway: People of color can also deal with white fragility.

Most black people say that they are willing to give feedback to white people, but the problem is that most white people cannot accept it. They refuse to own and fix their racist patterns. The best strategy is to find a white person you trust and ask them to point it out to the offender.

According to DiAngelo, people of color should not shoulder the burden of dealing with white fragility. It is whites who must learn to be racially aware.

EDITORIAL REVIEW

In her book *White Fragility*, Robin J. DiAngelo tackles the sensitive subject of racial equality in modern America. The book is an attempt to challenge white people to openly talk about racial equality instead of shrinking back from this topic.

She coined the term *White Fragility* when writing a peer-reviewed paper in 2011. The term white fragility refers to the defensive actions that white people take when they are placed under some racial stress. These defensive moves include arguing, walking away, playing the victim, or accusing the other person of racism.

One of the main concepts that she puts forth is the inaccurate view that white people have regarding racism. Whites think that only evil and uneducated people can be racist, but DiAngelo counters by saying that all white people are racist to some degree. This doesn't mean that all whites are evil. Her point is that due to the way they are socialized and brought up, they tend to view people of color as being inferior. As a result, a white person may say something that sounds normal but actually reinforces a racial stereotype.

For example, a white person tells another to avoid buying a house in a specific neighborhood because "you might need a gun to protect yourself." DiAngelo argues that white people use such coded words when referring to neighborhoods that are predominantly black.

DiAngelo uses many real-life examples to highlight just how pervasive racism is and how fragile white people are when challenged about it. For example, when a white teacher mocks a parent, everyone in the room can tell that she is referring to a black woman. When DiAngelo tells her that her statement is racist, the teacher is shocked by her accusation and almost suffers a nervous breakdown.

The book is written in a casual tone that makes it easy for the reader to keep up with the content. DiAngelo is an academic and often uses complex terms, but she manages to break down every concept that she puts forth. This book is meant to bring transformation at a personal and national level, and making the book easy to read helps to achieve that goal.

DiAngelo also incorporates a lot of content from other writers who have addressed the issue of race. She quotes acclaimed authors like Ta-Nehisi Coates, Eduardo Bonilla-Silva, Omowale Akintunde, and many others.

The topic of racism is one that has been tackled by many authors in the past, but what makes this book different is the way DiAngelo has revealed the concept of white supremacy. As a white person who has twenty years of experience teaching on racism and social justice, she is able to offer a unique perspective that drives the point home. This is not someone offering their personal opinion about an event. DiAngelo uses her own upbringing and socialization to show fellow whites that racism is a systemic and structural problem in America.

This is not DiAngelo's first attempt to write about racism in America. She has published two books that talk about social justice and how white people can improve their racial literacy. Her goal is to show white people that white fragility perpetuates racism. Instead of keeping silent or getting defensive, white people can help chip away at the racist structure by engaging in constructive dialogue with each other and people of color.

BACKGROUND ON AUTHOR

Robin J. DiAngelo is an American educator, academic, and author. Her primary fields of work are whiteness studies and critical discourse analysis. She has over twenty years of experience as a trainer and consultant on racial issues. She has also published two other books on the topic of racial equality and social justice.

Born in 1956, DiAngelo graduated from Washington University with a Ph.D. in Multicultural Education. By 2007, she was a lecturer at the Westfield State University, and in 2014, she became a professor of multicultural education in the same faculty. She later left her tenured professorship at Westfield and now lectures part-time at Washington University's School of Social Work. She has twice been awarded the Student's Choice Awards for Educator of the Year. She also works as the Equity Director for the Seattle-based Sound Generations.

Apart from her academic pursuits, DiAngelo often holds workshops and seminars where she discusses racial issues and how racism is deeply ingrained in American culture and politics. She coined the term "white fragility" in 2011 after writing a peer-reviewed thesis. The article was published in the *New York Times*, the *Atlantic*, *Colorlines*, and *Salon*.

DiAngelo currently lives in Seattle, Washington.

OTHER TITLES BY ROBIN DIANGELO

Is Everyone Really Equal?: An Introduction to Key Concepts in Social Justice Education (2012)

What Does It Mean to Be White?: Developing White Racial Literacy (2012)

END OF BOOK SUMMARY

*If you enjoyed this **ZIP Reads** publication, we encourage you to purchase a copy of the original book from.*

We'd also love an honest review on Amazon.com!

CPSIA information can be obtained
at www.ICGtesting.com
Printed in the USA
BVHW032156061218
535006BV00001B/99/P